MORE VIEWS OF OLD BARKING AND DAGENHAM

Compiled by
Susan Curtis
Jennifer Murphy
and
Mark Watson

1991

LIBRARIES DEPARTMENT
LONDON BOROUGH OF BARKING AND DAGENHAM

Introduction

The collection of items for a local history museum began during 1938. At this time, Valence House had ceased to be Dagenham Council's Administrative Centre and the building was re-used as the Headquarters of the Library Service.

J.G. O'Leary, Dagenham's charismatic Chief Librarian, was also an enthusiastic local historian and the illustrations collection he pioneered has been gathered from junk shops, antique fairs or by generous donations and loans from the general public. In 1888, when the first roll-film camera, backed up by a developing and printing service, was introduced photographs became much more accessible, and many images of our area survive from the late 19th century.

The Borough's extensive picture collection now includes many thousands of items. It is strong in photographs of local buildings and industrial sites, but is weaker in showing the social history of Barking and Dagenham.

Museum staff would like to redress this balance, and collect more photographs illustrating everyday family life in the Borough. We are happy to receive donations, or to copy items which the owner wants to retain. In this way, we hope to expand our holdings for the education and entertainment of future generations.

Susan Curtis
Jennifer Murphy
Mark Watson
Libraries and Museums Service
London Borough of Barking and Dagenham

Foreword

Following the success of the publication of "Views of Old Barking and Dagenham", the Libraries Department has decided to issue a further selection of views from its extensive photographic collection. There is a continuing demand for material illustrating the Borough's past and we are fortunate in having such a rich resource. It is hoped that further volumes, possibly of a more specialised nature, will follow.

I am grateful to those members of the staff in the Libraries Department who have compiled this volume and to those residents who have continued to give their encouragement and support.

Councillor T. M. Bird
Chairman of the Libraries Committee

CONTENTS

Cover Photograph:

Barking Court House. This charming photograph shows a group of children outside the Elizabethan Court House in Barking. Built in 1566/7, it used to contain the parish stocks, where drunk and disorderly citizens were temporarily confined.
The front of the building was in the Broadway, but this view shows residents in Back Lane. Unfortunately, this historical building was demolished in 1926.

Parsloes Manor House. The Manor of Parsloes is named after Hugh Passelewe, a 13th century owner. In 1619, the estate was purchased by William Fanshawe of Fanshawe Gate in Derbyshire. This house was owned by the Fanshawe family for 300 years. The building was derelict by the end of the 19th century, and was demolished in 1925. Part of the Parsloes estate is now a public park while the remainder is covered with council housing on the Becontree Estate.

1

Hunters Hall Farm. This farmhouse stood to the south of Oxlow Lane in Dagenham, opposite the end of Frizlands Lane. The farm was named after Robert Hunter, who was working on the land in 1609.

Joynes Cottages. Agricultural labourers employed at Dagenham farms in the Victorian period would have lived in small brick cottages like these in Oxlow Lane. this picturesque view dates from about 1920.

Rookery Farm. Rookery Farmyard in Bull Lane, Dagenham, 1933.

4

May Cottages. May Cottages, Becontree Heath, Dagenham, which was built in 1908 is seen here c.1920. Clay Cottages can be seen in the background. The path on the right of the picture leads to Wood Lane. The girl on the left is called Ethel St Pier.

5

Exterior of the barn, Warren Farm, Chadwell Heath, 1912. This barn is the only surviving building of the ancient Manor of Marks. It was constructed in the seventeenth century and is situated to the east of Whalebone Lane North, Chadwell Heath.

6

Interior of the barn, Warren Farm, Chadwell Heath, 1947/8. This red brick building has a fine beam roof with "arrow" slitted walls which provide good ventilation.

Eastbrook Farm, Dagenham, c.1929. This weather-boarded and thatched farmhouse was allowed to run down after its land was acquired for building by the London County Council.

In 1933, Dagenham Urban District Council built a Salvage Plant, from which waste materials could be re-used. This was a pioneer venture in the 1930's. This land now forms part of Central Park, Dagenham.

EASTBROOK END FARM DAGENHAM

Eastbrookend Farm, Dagenham, c.1920. This late 17th century farmhouse was situated immediately to the west of Eastbrookend House (now the Farmhouse public house in Dagenham Road). The farm has been demolished and the land is now in Central Park.

Mr Terry's piggery, Billet Lane, Marks Gate, 1948. Billet Lane is situated in the most northern part of the Parish of Dagenham at Marks Gate. This area was a quiet rural hamlet until development took place in the 1950's. In 1950, final approval was received for the construction of a new housing estate. Green Belt land was released by the Ministry of House Building , due to a local shortage of suitable land. The Marks Gate Housing Estate was officially opened in 1960, with Billet Lane as its northern boundary. The local artist, A. E. Baker, described the agricultural nature of Marks Gate, where "pigs were bred on most of the farms and provided the small farmer with his chief source of income".

East End Farmhouse, Workhouse Lane, Dagenham, c.1920. Numbers 61 and 63 Holgate Road, now stand on this site.

Starling's Hall Farm, Rippleside, Barking. c.1920. Rippleside is situated about 2 miles east of Barking town. In the foreground, in a farm wagon, are wooden reels from the Union Cable Company at Dagenham Dock.

GREAT PORTERS FARM BARKING

The farmyard at Great Porters, Barking. This farm was part of the ancient manorial estate of Porters. The Porter family are recorded as holding land in Barking Parish as early as 1220. Their name is currently preserved in Dagenham at Porters Avenue.

13

Peace Tea, Heath Street, Barking, 1918. The people of Barking organised street parties to celebrate the end of the Great War (1914 to 1918).

14

Dagenham Charter Ball, 1938. Civic dignitaries attending the charter ball at Dagenham County High School in October 1938. Dagenham's Charter celebrations were originally postponed due to international strife. Seated in the centre of the first row is the Mayor of Dagenham, Councillor A. F. J. Chorley.

15

The Chase at Eastbrookend, Dagenham, 1930's. Children are playing in disused gravel pits at The Chase. This area will form part of a new "Country Park".

16

Dagenham Cycling Club, c.1920s. These keen cyclists are seen outside the Chequers public house, New Road, Dagenham. This building was demolished in the late 1980's and Halford's store on the A13 now occupies this site.

Coronation Street Party, Monmouth Road, Dagenham, 1953. This street entertainment was part of Dagenham Town Carnival, on June 6th, which celebrated the coronation of Queen Elizabeth II. The Winsorettes, a local dance troupe, perform a nautical number. Notice the decorated house in the background.

Curfew F.C.

Curfew Football Club, Barking, 1910. This team were winners of the Manor Division (Barking and District) in the 1909 to 1910 season. The vicar of Barking, Reverend J. Eisdell, is pictured with the dog sitting on his lap on the left of the picture. This organisation eventually became Barking Town Football Club.

19

The Boating Lake, Barking Park, 1946. This Boating Lake was over half a mile long and about 100 feet wide. It was obviously a very popular family activity in April 1946, shortly after the end of World War II.

The Grange Cinema, Dagenham, c.1928. A works char-a-banc outing are seen outside the Grange Cinema, which was situated at the junction of Goresbrook Road and the Heathway. The current motion picture on show was "What Price Glory".

21

Valence Swimming Pool, 1932. This pool, serving the Becontree Housing Estate, was officially opened at this ceremony by Sir George Lansbury M.P. A celebrity guest, wearing the "England" costume, was Ted Temme. He was the first person to successfully swim the English Channel twice, and he also represented Great Britain in the Olympic Games of 1936.

This party for children was held to celebrate the signing of the Armistice which ended the Great War (1914 to 1918). The bunting is flying in Howard Road, Barking.

23

Ford Motor Company. Cutting the first turf on the site of the factory. 17.5.1929. The first Ford factory in England was opened in Manchester in 1911. This factory only assembled American vehicles. After the Great War, as demand grew, it became clear there was a need for a new factory specially designed for large scale production of British cars and the final choice of site was Dagenham.

Ford production line Model A Truck. The first vehicle to be produced in Dagenham, 1931. Four years after the first Dagenham built vehicle left the assembly line the £100 car was introduced. The lowest priced, fully equipped saloon car ever to be made by any manufacturer.

25

Discharging slag in ladles at the Ford Motor Company, Dagenham Dock.

Party visit to the Ford Motor Company, Dagenham, 1938. In 1938 the annual production of the Dagenham company was 87,000 cars, trucks and tractors. The famous Fordson tractor seen in the photograph was first used in Britain in 1917 and helped to make British agriculture the most mechanised in the world.

27

This traditional riverside scene shows Thames Sailing Barges in Barking Creek. On the quay stands Jackson and Company's premises. This well known firm is one of the oldest established businesses in Barking and was founded in 1874. It primarily supplied the building trade with bricks, lime, cement and sand.

28

The Town Quay Steam Wharf and Saw Mills, the Town Quay, Barking. A new office development now occupies this waterside site.

29

Gross, Sherwood and Heald Limited's Paint Factory, in Barking, 1910. The original factory was established in 1777 as manufacturers of oils and greases. Paint making was introduced as a small side line and developed into a large part of the business. In this picture men are seen packing various goods.

30

Gross, Sherwood and Heald Limited, Barking, 1910. The interior of the tin box factory.

31

Aerial view of the Union Cable Company Limited works at Dagenham Dock. The Union Cable Company came to Dagenham in 1900. By 1911, the factory, offices and warehouse occupied an eight acre site at Dagenham Dock. This enterprise is now called Telephone Cables Ltd., and is a major European manufacturer in the communications field.

Samuel Williams and Sons Limited, Dagenham Dock, c.1897. In 1887, Samuel Williams acquired hundreds of acres of land at Dagenham Breach. This area gradually developed into the vast industrial area we now know as Dagenham Dock. This photograph shows manual workers towards the close of the nineteenth century

33

Industrial Scene, Abbey Road, Barking, c.1900. In the yard of the Abbey Match Works, Jackson's horse-drawn delivery waggon can be seem. The tall building in the background is Randall's Malthouse, which was built in 1866.

The Regent Oil Company, Barking, c.1930. This company prepared specialised oil for industry using products from the West Indies, the United States, South America and the Middle East. Their ocean-going tankers were well known in the Thames Estuary.

35

The coaling jetty at Barking Power Station, Creekmouth, c.1948. This part of the River Thames frontage features in an ambitious development plan, including houses, shops and leisure amenities, at Barking Reach.

Waterlow and Sons Limited, Wantz Road, Dagenham, 1951. This printing company had several factories in London. It opened this branch in Dagenham in 1948. In 1951 it employed about 200 people who were manufacturing catalogues, guides and diaries.

Barking Tea Exchange, c.1910. The proprietor of this grocery store, Walter Leftley, is standing in the doorway. The business was originally established as a "Tea House" in 1833.

Jackson's horse-drawn waggon, Barking, c.1900. This scene in St Ann's Road shows Daniel Thomas Jackson in the foreground standing beside his Victorian delivery vehicle. In the 1880's Mr Jackson was a shopkeeper and grocer but by 1894 he is recorded as being a carman and contractor.

39

East Street, Barking, c.1928. An interesting scene showing the street before alterations, with the Wesleyan Chapel visible to the right. Outside Sander's Committee Rooms on the left, a poster urges residents to "Vote for Sanders". John Thomas Sanders was a local councillor for Central Ward who was elected as a County Councillor and became an Essex Alderman.

East Street, Barking, c.1937. A number 13 tramcar is featured in the foreground serving Barking's main shopping street. In the background the Capitol Cinema stands on the site vacated by Marks and Spencers in 1990. The current film was "Stella Dallas" directed by King Vidor.

41

Hollick's newsagents shop, 6, East Street, Barking, c.1927. John Hollick started delivering newspapers at the age of nine (c.1905) and eventually became the owner of six shops. The first shop opened c.1922 and the last of the chain in 1957, all were managed by members of the family.

42

The Linton Toilet Saloon, Linton Road, Barking, c.1920's. The old style of barber's shop is illustrated in this interior shot. The business was run by Robert Henry Goffin of Nethersfield Gardens, Barking, until his death in 1927.

43

The Broadway, Barking, c.1905. This busy shopping area was situated opposite the Curfew Tower. The town's historic market was sited in this thoroughfare.

44

Longbridge Road, Barking, c.1902. The Spotted Dog public house, in the centre of the picture, has been on this site since 1870. Some properties in this area were demolished c.1905 when the railway line was widened. The terrace of shops contained Worby's confectioner's and tobacconist's, John Hobb's dining rooms, William Crouch's general store, Mrs Ellis's laundry, Churchill's the butcher, Lee's fruit shop and the Essex Lead and Glass Company run by James Lewis.

45

Barking Market, c.1950's. This open market was situated near Barking Town Hall, on the way from East Street to Axe Street. The market was closed for town redevelopment.

46

The Old Curiosity Shop, Chadwell Heath, July 1914. This picturesque antiques shop, housed in a weather-boarded and thatched building, is shown in the summer sun shortly before the outbreak of the Great War.

47

East Street, Barking. c.1902. These properties, which stood on the south side of East Street, were required for railway clearance in 1905.

East Street, Barking, c.1924. The junction of Ripple Road and London Road, had recently been converted into a pedestrian precinct with the opening of Vicarage Field Shopping Centre. Barclay's Bank and the Brewery Tap still occupy the same sites.

49

Delivery Cart, Chadwell Heath Lane, 1953. This London Co-operative Society coal waggon is seen travelling from Romford to Chadwell Heath Station coal yard.

58

Street vendor, Becontree Housing Estate, c.1950. This trader is selling groceries from a pony-drawn cart in Dagenham.

51

Linton Road, Barking. c.1930. Looking north-west along Linton Road, the Brewery Tap public house is on the right. Glenny's Brewery was situated behind this building.

Church Elm Lane, Dagenham Village, c.1930. This parade of shops still exists, however, housing now fills the open ground to the right and there is a car park to the left.

53

Crown Street, Dagenham Village, c.1912. The building in the foreground, advertising the business of G. Bales and Sons, formerly housed the Rose and Crown public house.

Dagenham Village, 1948. Shops and cottages in Bull Street, which is now Rainham Road South. Cooper's Cafe was situated opposite the car park of the Bull public house.

New Road, Dagenham, 1936. On the right is the Princess Cinema, which is now a bowling alley. The tower of Marsh Green School is visible in the distance. The entrance to the Ford works is on the left.

Chadwell Heath High Road, c.1910. This historic way was the main Roman Road linking London and Colchester.

57

Ripple School, Suffolk Road, Barking. Built in 1913, Ripple School was one of the first single storey schools to be constructed in England.

Empire Day, Westbury School, 1908. The celebration of "Empire Day" was introduced in England on 24th May, 1902. Children dressed in costume representing various parts of the British Empire. This unusual view from the air shows the playground at Westbury School. This event was re-named Commonwealth Day in 1959.

59

Barking Church of England School, c.1912. This Edwardian picture shows girls at Barking's oldest school. They are creating a tableau of St Margaret, patron saint of Barking Parish Church.

North Street School, Barking, 1907. Mixed pupils take part in traditional Maypole dancing in the hall. This celebration took place on the 24th July, the last day of the summer term in 1907.

61

Standard 2 at the Church of England School, Barking, c.1910. The young girls were encouraged to wear white smocks for special occasions, such as a visit from the local photographer.

Boys of class 5, Westbury School, Barking, c.1930. This school was built in 1904. The teachers in this picture, from left to right, are Mr Stevenson, Mr Tibbenham and Mr Martin.

63

The staff at Green Lane School, Chittys Lane, Dagenham, c.1940. In the centre of the front row is Henry Green, who was the Headmaster from 1925 to 1946. He became an Essex County Councillor and offered considerable expertise as chairman of the Education Committee. This school is now named "Henry Green School" in honour of his life and work.

Becontree Heath School, Dagenham, 1950. Formal-style lesson in progress with a mixed class.

Girls of class 7, Northbury School, Barking, c.1920. This Victorian school, constructed in 1896, was described in the periodical "London" as "one of the best board schools in the country".

Gascoigne Road School, 1925. The boys of class III are pictured with two teachers. This school was built in 1892. In the background, the School Honours Board is seen on display.

Grafton Junior School, Becontree Avenue, Dagenham, c.1950. A mixed group of junior school pupils participate in a physical education session. This school on the Becontree Housing Estate opened in 1928, and was re-organised for infants and juniors in 1935.

Eastbrook School, Dagenham, 1949. Eastbrook School for girls and boys opened in 1934. Pupils wearing smart uniforms are learning how to bake cakes under the supervision of the domestic science teacher.

69

The Ford Endowed School, Dagenham. This school was founded under the will of William Ford, a Dagenham farmer, who died in 1825. He left £10,000 in trust to the parish churchwardens and overseers to establish a school for 30 boys and 20 girls. The Trustees later opened a second school in Whalebone Lane.

The Bull Inn, Rainham Road South, Dagenham, c.1900. A building has been on this site since at least the 17th century. The first record mentioning "The Bull" dates from 1726. In the 19th century, the Bull's importance grew with the development of travel and communications. By 1848, the Rainham Omnibus was calling at this pub each morning at nine o'clock on its journey to London.

71

The Robin Hood Inn, Bennetts Castle Lane, Dagenham, 1920. In 1851, James Bigsby ran a beer shop in Bennetts Castle Lane. Ten years later this was known as the Robin Hood and Little John. In 1886 it was only called the Robin Hood and by 1969 it had become the Peoples' Dispensary for Sick Animals.

The Robin Hood, Longbridge Road, c.1930. The new Robin Hood public house was built between 1929 and 1933.

73

The George Inn, The Broadway, c.1880. The George was an old coaching inn, prior to 1854 the pub's owner, Mr White drove a coach twice daily to the Bull at Aldgate. James Holmes took possession in 1856. He died in 1881 and this building was demolished in c.1892.

The 'Who'd have thought it' public house, Axe Street, Barking, 1929. This public house in central Barking was converted into a private club in 1964. The building is still standing.

75

The Chadwell Arms public house, High Road, Chadwell Heath, c.1930. A char-a-banc outing showing members of a skittle group standing outside the Chadwell Arms. Note the cobbled street and tram lines in the foreground.

The Victoria public house, Axe Street, Barking, c.1940. This small establishment was situated opposite the "Who'd have thought it" in Axe Street. This building was demolished, and a new public house, named the Victoria, was constructed in 1961.

77

The Cross Keys Public House, Crown Street, Dagenham. This is the oldest secular building in Dagenham, and dates from about 1500. Originally a timber-framed house, it became a village inn called "The Queen's Head" in 1700, and acquired its present name before 1785.

The Ship and Anchor public house, Becontree Heath, c.1935.

79

The Jolly Fisherman public house, North Street, Barking. c.1930. This beer house was built in 1906 and the name reflects the major industry relating to Barking town.

The Crooked Billet, Creekmouth, Barking, c.1940. Originally, this public house was a small, wooden house which was enlarged at a later date. The establishment was well patronised by the Barking fishermen. This picture shows a Royal Air Force crew who were engaged in winching up barrage balloons in Barking during World War II.

The Three Travellers public house, Becontree Heath, 1964. In 1819, this establishment was known as "The Travellers Inn" but by 1840, the name had been changed to "The Three Travellers".

The Barge Aground, The Broadway, Barking, 1972. These buildings near the Curfew Tower were demolished c.1973, shortly after this photograph was taken. There has been an establishment bearing the name "The Barge Aground" in the town since at least 1662, when it was described as being a "beer house". The present Barge Aground stands on the opposite side of the road to the building pictured near to the Broadway Theatre.

83

Carnival in Barking Park, August 1909. Daniel Poulter was a cowkeeper and shopkeeper of 2 Harpour Road, Barking.

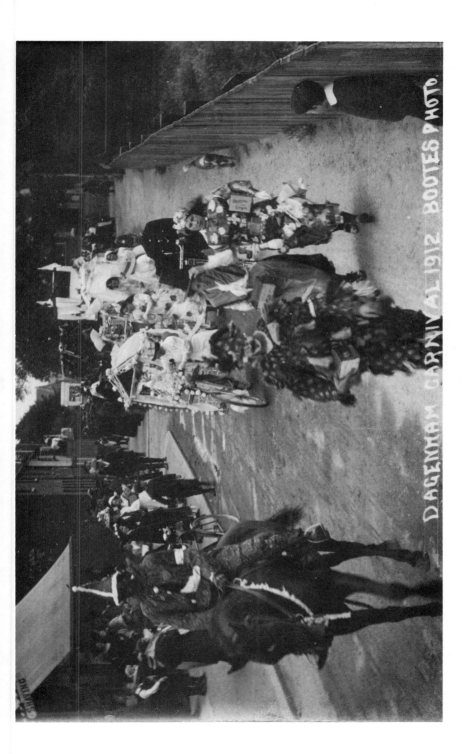

Carnival Procession in Church Street, Dagenham, 1912. Dagenham Parish Church is visible in the background.

85

Barking Charter Pageant, 1931. Six performances of this spectacular pageant took place between Monday October 5th and Saturday October 10th, 1931. This picture shows members of Barking Bowling Club participating in Scene 10, which features King Charles II (who was restored to the English throne in 1660) and his courtiers.

Barking Charter Celebrations, 1931. Flags, bunting and the people of Barking welcome the horse-drawn coach transporting the Lord Mayor of London. It is seen arriving at the Public Offices (now Barking Magistrates Court) in East Street on October 6th.

Labour Celebration, 1937. The women's section of Barking Labour Party are seen demonstrating against the means test on May Day, 1937. The means test was introduced in 1931. The Ministry of Labour was not equipped to carry out the test. This work was entrusted to Public Assistance Committees of local councils. Labour councils, such as Barking and Dagenham, either refused to carry out the means test or carried it out in an evasive manner.

Coronation Day, Barking, 12th May, 1937. To mark the coronation of King George VI, 1,330 parcels were given to residents of the Borough of Barking aged over 70. This ceremony took place outside the Public Offices in East Street.

Ministry of Food Van, 1947. This publicity van was sent to the Borough as it was feared that only half the children in Dagenham were receiving their ration of cod liver oil and orange juice.

Pipe Major Charles Cameron and the Dagenham Girl Pipers Band. The Dagenham Girl Pipers held their first practice session on the 4th of October, 1930.

91

Road Safety Exhibition, 1947. Display produced by Dagenham Urban District Council's Road Safety Department recreating the horror of a car accident. The official on the right, wearing a bow-tie, is Alderman William E. Bellamy.

Industrial Exhibition, Barking, 1st October, 1930. This display formed part of the town's Charter Celebrations. This imaginative stand shows the amount of timber and boxes required for half an hour's full production of matches at J. John Masters and Company Limited, Abbey Match Works, Barking.

93

Procession during Civic Day in Dagenham, 1931.

Barking Carnival, 1960. Barking Youth Council's decorated float.